AF585275

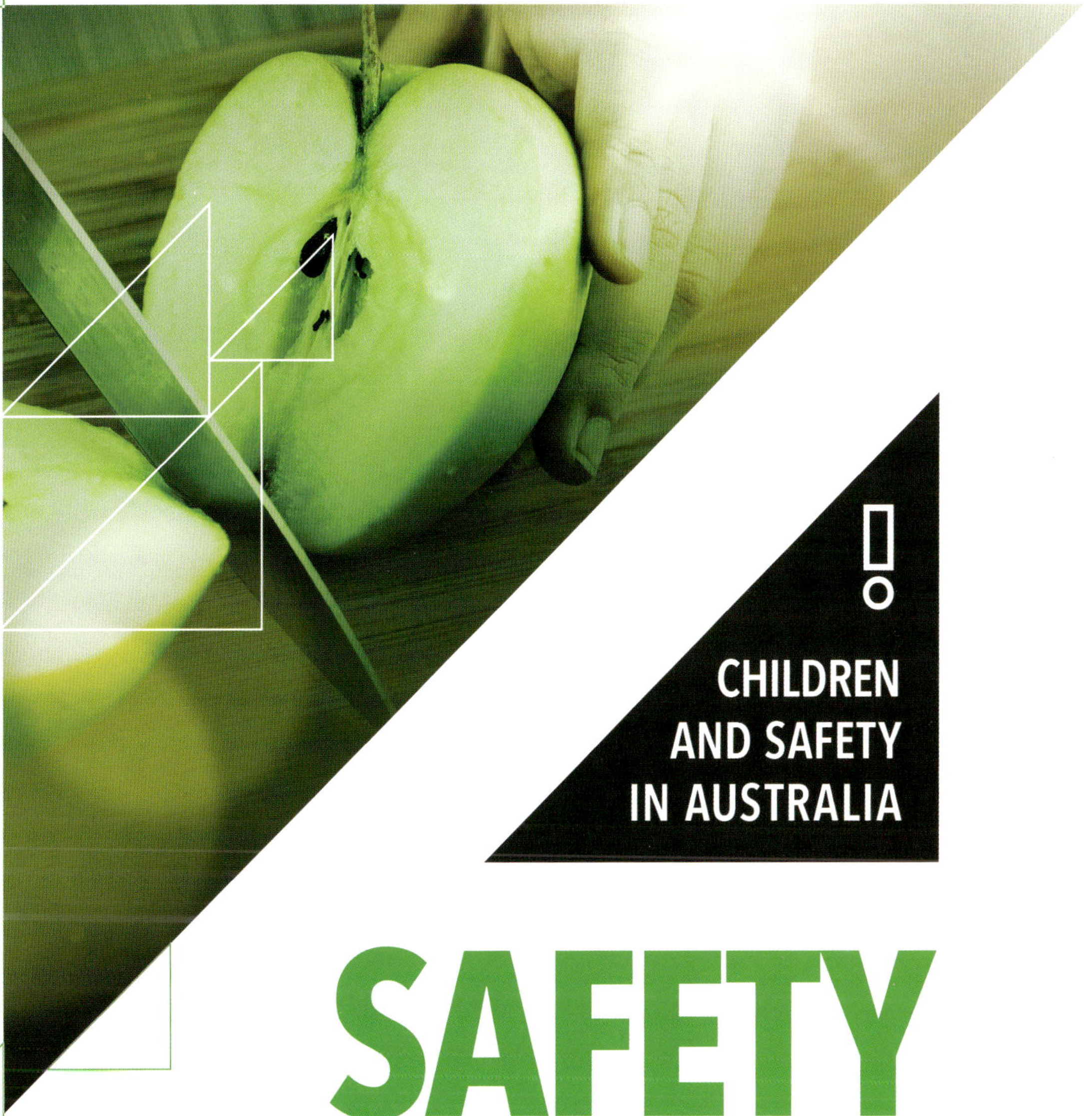

CHILDREN AND SAFETY IN AUSTRALIA

SAFETY AT HOME

WILLIAM DAY

Redback Publishing
PO Box 357 Frenchs Forest NSW 2086
Australia

www.redbackpublishing.com.au
orders@redbackpublishing.com.au

978-1-925630-65-7

Author: William Day
Editor: Marianne Lindsell
Designer: Redback Publishing

Original illustrations © Redback Publishing 2018
Originated by Redback Publishing

Printed and bound in China by Leo Paper

Acknowledgements
Abbreviations: l—left, r—right, b—bottom, t—top, c—centre, m—middle
We would like to thank the following for permission to reproduce photographs:
(Images © shutterstock)

Every effort has been made to contact copyright holders of any material reproduced in this book. Any omissions will be rectified in subsequent printings if notice is given to the publisher.

A catalogue record for this book is available from the National Library of Australia

CONTENTS

INTRODUCTION

Home is a place where children should be able to feel completely safe and happy. There are many things that can interfere with the safety of a child at home, ranging from dangerous parts of buildings, to harmful acts by other people.

Children and adults can lessen all these threats to safety by being aware of what they are, and then knowing what actions they can take to reduce the dangers, or remove them altogether.

Older children can play an important role by looking after the safety of younger brothers and sisters at home. While it is the responsibility of parents to 'toddler-proof' their homes, so that little children are not exposed to dangers, older brothers and sisters can help by always being aware of what little children are doing. Help them to move out of harm's way if necessary, and then quickly tell a parent or trusted adult about the danger that needs to be fixed.

Young visitors to your home will like to explore the new surroundings. If you don't have any little children at home normally, then there may be dangers for your visitors. Help the adults at home by being aware of what toddlers are doing. Think ahead to what might happen if they get near an open window, the stove, hot water taps or anything else that could harm them.

EMERGENCY SERVICES IN AUSTRALIA

POLICE
State and territory governments in Australia provide their own police services.

AMBULANCE
Paramedics train on the job and by undertaking courses.

FIRE AND RESCUE SERVICES
Highly trained fire fighters respond to emergencies and provide information services for members of the public.

RURAL FIRE SERVICES
These services depend on their volunteer fire fighters.

CAREFLIGHT
An air ambulance service that uses the skills of doctors, nurses, paramedics and pilots.

AUSTRALIAN MARITIME SAFETY AUTHORITY
Provides search and rescue services at sea, as well as management of major ocean pollution incidents.

POISONS INFORMATION LINE
Call 13 11 26 from anywhere in Australia.

EMERGENCY ALERT
Emergency Alert is a government service that is sometimes used to alert people to an emergency in their area. The alert is sent by a voice message over a landline telephone, or by a text message to a mobile phone. The service may not always reach every person in an area and is only used in some circumstances.

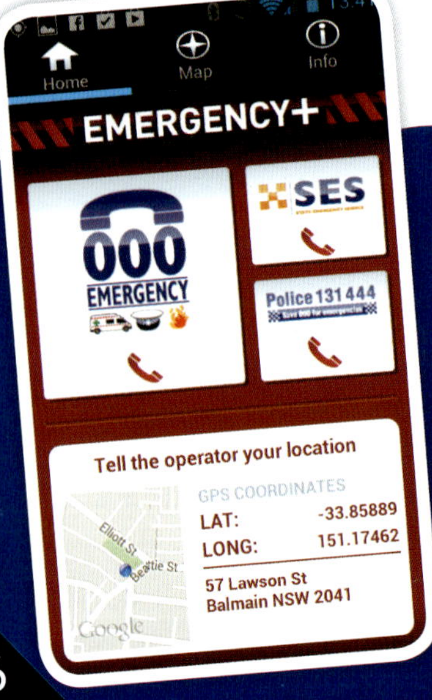

Emergency+ app

Emergency+ is a free app produced by Australia's emergency services. It uses your phone's GPS system to show on the screen exactly where you are. You can then tell the emergency service your location when you make the 000 call from the app.

HOW TO CONTACT EMERGENCY SERVICES IN AUSTRALIA

DO NOT DIAL 911

Have you watched movies and TV shows made in the USA in which people dial 911 for emergencies? This number does not work in Australia, where the emergency number to use is 000.

1. Dial 000 for police, ambulance and fire brigade.
2. Calmly tell them what is wrong.
3. They will ask where you are. If you do not know the address, tell them as much information as you know.
4. Do not end the call until they tell you to do so.

Dialling 000 from a mobile phone in Australia will still work even if there is no credit left on the phone. You can also make a free 000 call from any pay-phone in Australia.

If you are in a remote location where there is no mobile phone signal, your call will not connect. Anyone going into a remote area should think about getting a mobile satellite phone. This will let them make calls using a satellite connection rather than using signals sent to mobile phone towers. Geolocation emergency devices are available from park rangers in some of Australia's national parks. If a person is bushwalking or camping in a remote area, the geolocator may be the only way to contact emergency services.

STRANGER DANGER AT HOME

The rules about Stranger Danger apply at home as well as when you are away from home.

A Stranger at the Front Door

Strangers should not ask you to let them into your home. If they do, be very suspicious and close the door immediately. Then quickly tell the adults at home what has happened. Children should avoid answering the front door at any time.

A Stranger on the Phone

If you are allowed to answer the telephone when it rings, either the home phone or a mobile, there are a few rules that children should follow:

Don't tell anyone your name or address. The exception to this is if you have to ring the 000 emergency number and you are speaking to a person from the police, ambulance or fire brigade services.

Never tell a stranger that there is no adult at home with you.

If a stranger starts asking lots of other questions, just end the call right away. You do not have to speak to strangers on the phone.

Strangers seeking to do harm will tell lies. Be careful about believing what they say.

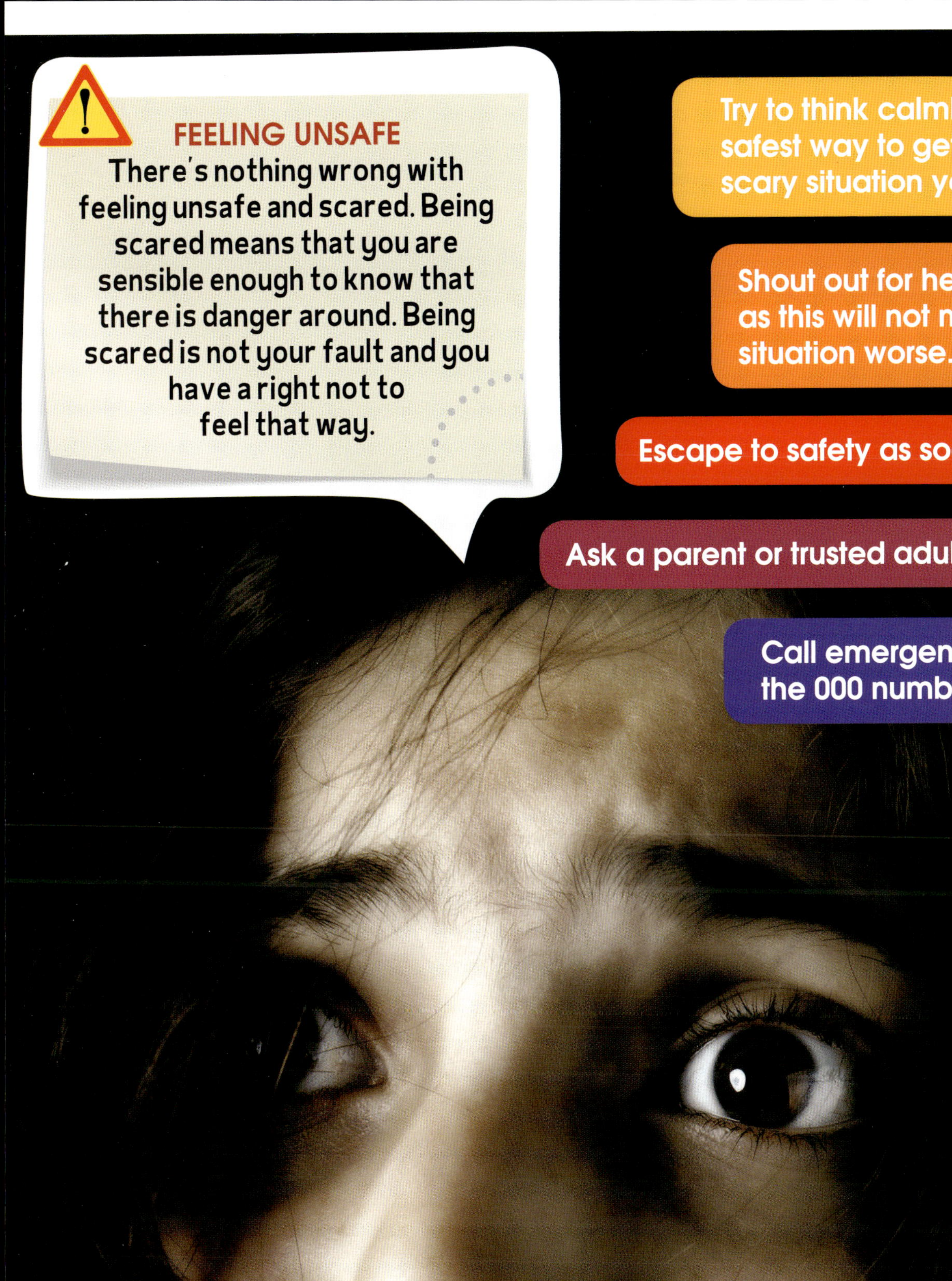

FEELING UNSAFE

There's nothing wrong with feeling unsafe and scared. Being scared means that you are sensible enough to know that there is danger around. Being scared is not your fault and you have a right not to feel that way.

Try to think calmly about the safest way to get out of the scary situation you are in.

Shout out for help as long as this will not make the situation worse.

Escape to safety as soon as you can.

Ask a parent or trusted adult to help you.

Call emergency services on the 000 number if necessary.

CARING FOR OTHERS
DISABLED CHILDREN AND ELDERLY RELATIVES

Children who have a disabled brother or sister can contribute to making everyone's lives happier by being aware of any safety issues around the home. Even though a disabled brother or sister may be older than you, they probably cannot always look after their own safety. Watch out for them wheeling their wheelchair too close to a heater, or check to see that they are alright if they have been alone for a while. The adults at home will really appreciate your help.

Elderly family members may also need your help around the home. Suffering a serious injury from falling over is something that happens to elderly people far too often. You can reduce the possibility of this happening by not leaving your toys where others can trip over them. Pick up toys that younger children have left around too.

Elderly people may have problems holding things securely because of arthritis in their hands. Holding a hot cup of tea can be dangerous if a person has a lot of pain in their hands. You can help by asking your elderly relatives if they want you to get anything for them.

SAFETY IN THE KITCHEN

The kitchen is the place where many families spend most of their time at home. There are many safety rules to know about in the kitchen. Toddlers who cannot understand these rules need to be protected so they do not get near the many dangerous implements and machines that we use in kitchens. If there is a toddler in your home, be aware that they cannot predict danger in the same way that older children can. If you open toddler-proof cupboards or move a child security gate, quickly put them all back the way they were so that little children do not come to any harm.

KITCHEN DANGERS

Glass

Broken glass needs to be cleaned away by an adult as soon as possible. Tiny slivers of glass may spread all across the floor and stick into the skin on bare feet. These are very difficult to pull out because they are almost invisible. If your parent is busy cleaning up the broken glass, it will be up to you to keep your little brother or sister away from the kitchen until it is safe for them to walk on the floor again.

Toasters

What would you do if a piece of toast became stuck in the toaster? Hopefully you would never stick a metal knife in it to get the bread out! Doing this can cause a person to receive an electric shock which might be life threatening. This would be a terrible outcome when all you want to do is eat a piece of toast. If you are allowed to use electrical appliances at home, what you should do is turn the toaster off at the wall switch and pull the plug out of the socket before attempting to get the bread out. Otherwise, ask an adult at home to help you.

Knives

We need knives to prepare food but they can be dangerous if children use them in the wrong way. Never leave a knife on a bench or table where a toddler can pick it up. Ask an adult at home to show you the correct way to cut food with a kitchen knife so that you avoid harming yourself. One of the skills you need to learn is how to cut away from yourself rather than sliding the knife towards your hand.

Pots on the Stove

A pot on the stove with a handle sticking out over the edge is a danger to children. Toddlers will try to pull the handle down to see what is inside the pot. Even an adult could knock the handle as they walk past and tip the hot contents of the pot onto the ground.

If you see that the stove has been switched on by mistake, particularly if a toddler has been playing near it, tell an adult and turn the stove off.

Kettles

The cord of a kettle is like a rope toy to a toddler. If it is hanging over the edge of the kitchen bench, a toddler will try to pull on the cord and could receive a terrible injury. Keep all cords from electrical appliances out of their reach.

Reaching a High Shelf

If you need to reach something that is on a high shelf, ask an adult to get it for you. It may be on that shelf because it is a poison or because it is something you are not allowed to have. Climbing on the kitchen bench or on chairs to reach high shelves is not a good idea. As you lean over to reach what you want to get, the chair could tip or your foot might slip on a soapy or wet surface.

Refrigerators

Keep the refrigerator door closed. Pets or even toddlers could try to climb inside to get food or to hide. If the door is left open, food inside will get warm and may be ruined.

FOOD SAFETY AT HOME

Some foods keep in the cupboard for months, while others only last a few hours before they become inedible. How can you tell which ones are safe to eat?

Meat and Fish

Meat must be kept cold in the refrigerator. If a piece of raw meat is left out on the kitchen bench, bacteria growing on it will quickly make it start to decay.

FOOD COULD MAKE YOU SICK IF …

- it smells bad
- it looks the wrong colour
- it tastes strange
- it has been left out in the sun or another warm place for too long
- flies have been sitting on it or you can see insects crawling in it
- someone with dirty hands has touched it

Milk, Cream and Cheese

Dairy foods will go bad if they are not kept cold.

Eggs

Eggs need to be kept cool but not frozen. Sometimes there is just one bad egg in a whole carton of eggs, but you usually cannot tell which one this is just by looking at the shell. If you are cracking eggs into a bowl, you could crack each one into a separate container to check it is fresh before adding it to the rest.

Fruit and Vegetables

Fruit has its own natural packaging. The skin on fresh fruit provides a barrier to damage by insects, bacteria and mould. Producers of fruit sometimes spray it with chemicals to make it last longer, sc always wash the skin before you eat the fruit.

Have you ever seen white fuzz growing on strawberries, or the blue colour on orange skins? These are examples of moulds, tiny living things that cause food to decay. Mould ha: microscopic threads that reach into the fruit from the surface Once you see mould on the skin of fruit, you will need to either throw the fruit away, or cut out a large part of it.

Vegetables decay due to mould and drying out. Leafy vegetabl need to be kept in the refrigerator. Potatoes will turn green if the are exposed to sunlight. Eating green potatoes can make you sick.

ackaged Foods

ood that comes in packaging usually has preservatives added to it to make it last or a long time on shelves in shops and in your kitchen cupboards. The invention of reservatives has made more food available to people all around the world. Some reservatives are harmful if you eat too much of them. Fresh food is best.

read

heck bread for blue or black mould growing on it. Mouldy bread should e thrown away. There is nothing you can do to it to make it edible.

In Australia, people selling packaged food must add either a USE-BY DATE or a BEST-BY DATE to the outside of the package.

USE-BY DATES
After this date, food should not be sold and may be dangerous to eat.

BEST-BY DATES
After this date, food can still be sold as long as it is fit to eat, but it may not be of very good quality.

Choking dangers for babies and toddlers

Little children can choke on tiny lollies or pieces of hard food. Don't leave your packets of sweets or any other foods around where a toddler can reach them.

Allergies

If only one person in your family is allergic to a food, such as peanuts or milk, the whole family needs to be careful about sharing what they eat. Little children will be upset if they are not allowed to have something they see their big brothers and sisters eating. Try not to eat things in front of them that you know they cannot have because of their allergies.

It's too hot!

Check that drinks and soups are not too hot before you take a mouthful. If you leave a hot drink unattended, a little child may try to take a sip and burn their mouth. Try to keep any hot foods well out of their reach. A container of anything hot is very dangerous if a toddler tries to pull it down from a bench to see what is inside.

HOT!

SAFETY IN THE BATHROOM AND LAUNDRY

Bath toys and bubble bath turn bathrooms into places to play and relax. There are many dangers in the bathroom, and taking a little extra care will keep bath-time safe and fun.

Bathrooms

Water and soap on the floor makes the tiles slippery. Don't run or jump around in the bathroom, and hold onto the edge of the bath when climbing in or out of it.

Babies and toddlers can drown in the bath. Keep an eye on your little brothers and sisters to make sure they are not trying to fill up a bath by themselves and then getting in to play in the water.

Water and electricity are a disastrous combination! Don't use a hairdryer near water in the bathroom. If you drop it into a sink or bath full of water, someone could receive a serious electric shock.

The hot water tap can spurt out water that burns the skin. Turn the cold water tap on first, and then use the hot water tap.

Adults often keep medicines in bathroom cupboards. Keep the cupboard doors closed so that little children cannot get the medicines out and try to swallow them.

Laundries

Close the lids and doors of washing machines and dryers so that little children and pets don't try to crawl into them. Pets find the warm clothes inside a dryer very comfortable and might fall asleep on them if the door has been left open. If the door has to be left open to cool down and air the inside of the machine, keep the laundry door closed. If you need to get something out of the laundry, close the door when you leave so that your pets and younger siblings are kept safe.

The laundry is often the place where adults keep household poisons and cleaning products. We all know that little children will try to drink anything that is in a bottle, so the laundry is a dangerous place for them. Older children should be careful too. Some ordinary cleaning products can burn your eyes and skin, and make breathing difficult. A product in a bottle may look like water but it could be lethal.

WINDOWS AT HOME

If you sleep on the top of a double-decked bunk bed, you may be tempted to prop your pillow against the window. Although windows seem secure, never lean against the glass in case it either breaks or falls out of the frame.

Clear glass doors should have markings on them so that people do not walk right into the glass. Although all of your family will be familiar with where the doors are, visitors might not see them and then injure themselves when they bump against the glass.

Toddlers cannot yet understand how dangerous it is to lean out of windows, or to push against flyscreens. Talk to the adults at home about moving chairs, tables and beds away from windows so that toddlers cannot climb up and get near open windows. Window locks that only allow a window to open a safe distance should be attached if there are little children in the home. People living in apartments in some parts of Australia must have these sorts of locks on their windows.

The cords hanging down from blinds can be a danger if toddlers play with them. They could wrap the cord around themselves so that they cannot breathe. Cords should be attached high enough so that toddlers cannot touch them. If you open or close a blind, always put the cord back out of reach of little children.

POWER SOURCES

Power for light, heat, cooking and technology comes into our homes in various ways. All power sources have dangers and children need to know the safety rules for using power sensibly.

Electricity

Electricity comes into homes via wires, either from a large energy provider who supplies it to lots of people, or from a solar panel or a diesel motor kept outside.

We use electricity by plugging appliances into power points or by switching on lights. Electricity is lethal if used wrongly. Metal, water, electricity and people can be a dangerous combination. Never try to open up an electrical appliance to see what is inside. If it is still plugged in and switched on, such as a television on stand-by power, you could be electrocuted. Some electrical appliances are dangerous even if they are not switched on. They may have a capacitor inside that stores electrical energy. This can give you an electric shock.

If there is water on the floor, avoid touching any electrical appliance until the floor is cleaned up. An electrical appliance that falls into water and is switched on will make all the water a source of an electric shock if you touch it.

Gas

Gas used for stoves and heaters comes into a house through pipes from a large gas provider, or from gas bottles provided by the homeowner. Gas is explosive, which means it will catch on fire. If you see little children playing with the controls on a gas stove or heater, tell the adults at home. If you have learned how to use the controls yourself, check that the gas appliance is safe. Even if the gas does not ignite and cause a fire, the gas can be lethal to people in a closed area. Gas has an unpleasant odour, so if it is leaking out of a heater or a pipe, you will be able to smell it. Tell an adult at home right away if you smell a gas leak.

Gas bottles have controls which can turn the gas on and off. If you think they do not look the way they should, tell an adult at home immediately. Large gas bottles are sometimes used by houses in areas that do not have a gas supply coming from pipes laic under the road outside. Small gas bottles are more often used for BBQ cooking.

Open fires

Fireplaces with open fires were once in almost every home. Children would learn the dangers of fire from a very young age. Today, open fires in homes are rare. Children and visitors to the home may not know the fire safety rules as well as children did in the past.

An open fire is not something to play with. Hot ashes and embers can be very dangerous if they fall on anything flammable in the room.

Candles

Electricity has only been a source of lighting in Australian houses from the late 1800s. Before this, for many centuries, candles were the main source of light at night.

Today we use candles to enjoy their pleasant light and added perfume. Remember that candles are not toys. A candle will start a fire if the flame gets anywhere near something flammable, like clothes, curtains or carpets.

Batteries

Batteries in mobile phones and other equipment can be dangerous if treated in the wrong way. A battery can explode if it is in a fire. A mobile phone battery can cause a fire if the phone is damaged badly by being crushed.

SWIMMING POOLS

If younger children ask you to open a pool gate for them, would you do it?
Your answer should be NO!

Pool safety depends on everyone in the family, and visitors, all looking after younger children who do not realise that there could be danger if they are in or near the pool by themselves.

If the adults at home have told you not to use the pool except when you have their permission, there is a good reason for this. Children have drowned in backyard pools.

Keep away from the areas where the pool chemicals are stored at home. Chlorine is used in many pools to keep the water clean. It can cause severe burns and breathing problems if you get near it before it has been diluted properly in the pool water.

What if your neighbour has a pool that you really want to use?
Never enter another person's pool without permission both from them and your own parents or guardians. It is against the law to enter another person's yard if you have not been invited there.

If you go into your neighbour's pool secretly, there will be no-one to help you or other children with you if you get into trouble in the water.

The Royal Life Saving Society of Australia has a list of pool safety rules that everyone with a pool in their yard should know about. Did you know that they recommend tying up long hair when swimming, to stop it getting caught in the pool pumping system or other equipment?

There's a spider on the bottom of the pool!

If you scoop a spider out of the pool, or dive down to have a look at one in the water, take care. A spider can survive underwater for a while and it may still be alive.

Floating around on an inflatable pool toy is very relaxing and great fun. Anyone who cannot swim should not use these toys, just in case they deflate. Little children using inflatable floating aids, or floaties, are also at risk if the floatie gets a hole in it.

Baby splash pools are not safe just because the water level is low. Little children who slip in the splash pool can drown in a small amount of water. Portable pools with water only 30 cm deep need to have an approved safety fence around them in most parts of Australia.

SAFETY IN THE GARDEN

Garden Ponds

In many parts of Australia, any garden pond that is more than 30 cm deep needs to have an approved fence around it. This applies to fish ponds as well as swimming pools or spas. Little children love to lean over the edge of a fish pond to see what is going on under the water, or to feed the fish. Be a caring big brother or sister by watching to check that they do not fall in.

Bees and Wasps

An angry bee or wasp will sting anyone who gets near it. Avoid them as much as possible. People who are allergic to bee or wasp stings can have a severe reaction. They may need to use their Epipen, or go to hospital in an ambulance.

If you find a bee or wasp nest, keep away from it. Wasps have excellent eyesight, and sometimes will fly out of their nest to attack anyone walking near it.

Spiders, Snakes and Snails

Wear garden gloves if you are digging in the soil to plant a garden. Trapdoor spiders, funnel-web spiders, redback spiders and white-tailed spiders are all poisonous and can live in gardens.

If you see a snake in your garden, don't go near it to have a look. Most garden snakes will avoid humans, but they will react aggressively if they feel threatened. Native snakes are protected animals in Australia.

Little children love to put all sorts of unusual things in their mouths. If your little sibling puts a snail in their mouth, tell the adults at home right away, as some snails carry diseases which can spread to humans.

Garden Tools

awn mowers should only be used while an adult is supervising. People mowing ne lawn, whether they are adults or children, should wear strong shoes and oggles. Lawn mowers throw out more than just cut grass. They can toss sharp ieces of wood or metal up near your face.

lectric garden tools cause many injuries across Australia every year. Take care that ne electricity cord is not lying on the ground where it can be cut. This could result n people receiving an electric shock. Shout to warn an adult if you see they are bout to run over an electric cord with a lawn mower.

igging tools, saws and garden clippers are tools that should only be used nder adult supervision. If you are clipping a hedge, do you know what is n the other side of it before you start cutting? Toddlers and pets may un over to come and have a look at what you are doing, so be careful o keep them well away when you start cutting, sawing or igging with a spade.

Ladders

Children should not be climbing up ladders. Ladders are not toys, and there are many safety rules that adults need to follow when they use them. Unlike playground equipment, ladders are not securely fixed to something, and they can easily topple over.

Is There a Car in the Driveway?

When a driver is moving a car on the driveway, they may not be able to see children. Never run in front of or behind a car that is about to move, as you cannot rely on the driver seeing you and stopping. Toddlers will not understand the danger from cars, so keep an eye on them if they are in the garden with you.

Climbing Trees

- Do the adults at home allow you to climb trees in the garden?
- Will the branch hold your weight? Can you get down easily?
- Is there an adult at home who can help if you get stuck?
- Is there a magpie nest in the tree? If there is, the magpies will attack if you get near them.

PETS AT HOME

Pets are part of the family, and we sometimes like to treat them as though they are people. Having a pet is a lifetime responsibility, and it is up to the owner to look after their pet's health and welfare.

There are some aspects of pet ownership that can create dangerous situations at home for their owners and visitors.

Angry pets

Even the tiniest dogs are descended from wild wolves, and they still have some of the wild characteristics in their behaviour.

Dogs defend their territory, which to them is your home. If a stranger arrives and a dog is not sure if the person is allowed in the home, it might bark at them or even attack them. Dogs with this sort of instinct may attack anyone they don't know, including other dogs or even a little baby. If you have an angry dog at home, it is the owner's responsibility to make sure it is kept away from anyone it might want to attack.

Angry cats scratch to make people move away from them. Little children will want to feel the cat's soft fur, but a cat could see this as a threat and try to scratch or bite. If you have an angry cat, keep it away from little visitors and warn them not to pat it.

Protecting puppies and kittens

A mother dog that has puppies will become very protective of them. She may growl at you and not let you go near them. Ask the adults at home the best way to behave when you are near the mother dog and her puppies. A mother cat may also become aggressive if you try to touch her kittens.

Worms and germs

Dogs and cats that are allowed to be outside may eat things that give them worms in their intestines. Many of these worms can be transferred to humans by touching the dog or its droppings. Make sure the dog and the whole family stay healthy by giving the dog worm medicine regularly.

Cats' droppings contain all sorts of germs that can infect humans. If it is your job to change the cat litter at home, wash your hands carefully afterwards.

Always wash your hands after playing with your pet.

Birds

Parrots have strong beaks and will bite if you annoy or frighten them. Bird cages need to be cleaned regularly and the food and water should always be fresh. Wash your hands after cleaning the cage.

HOW SAFE ARE YOUR TOYS?

Product Safety Australia is the government body responsible for alerting consumers to unsafe toys.

Toy safety in Australia relies on everyone involved in their production, sale and use being aware of any possible dangers.

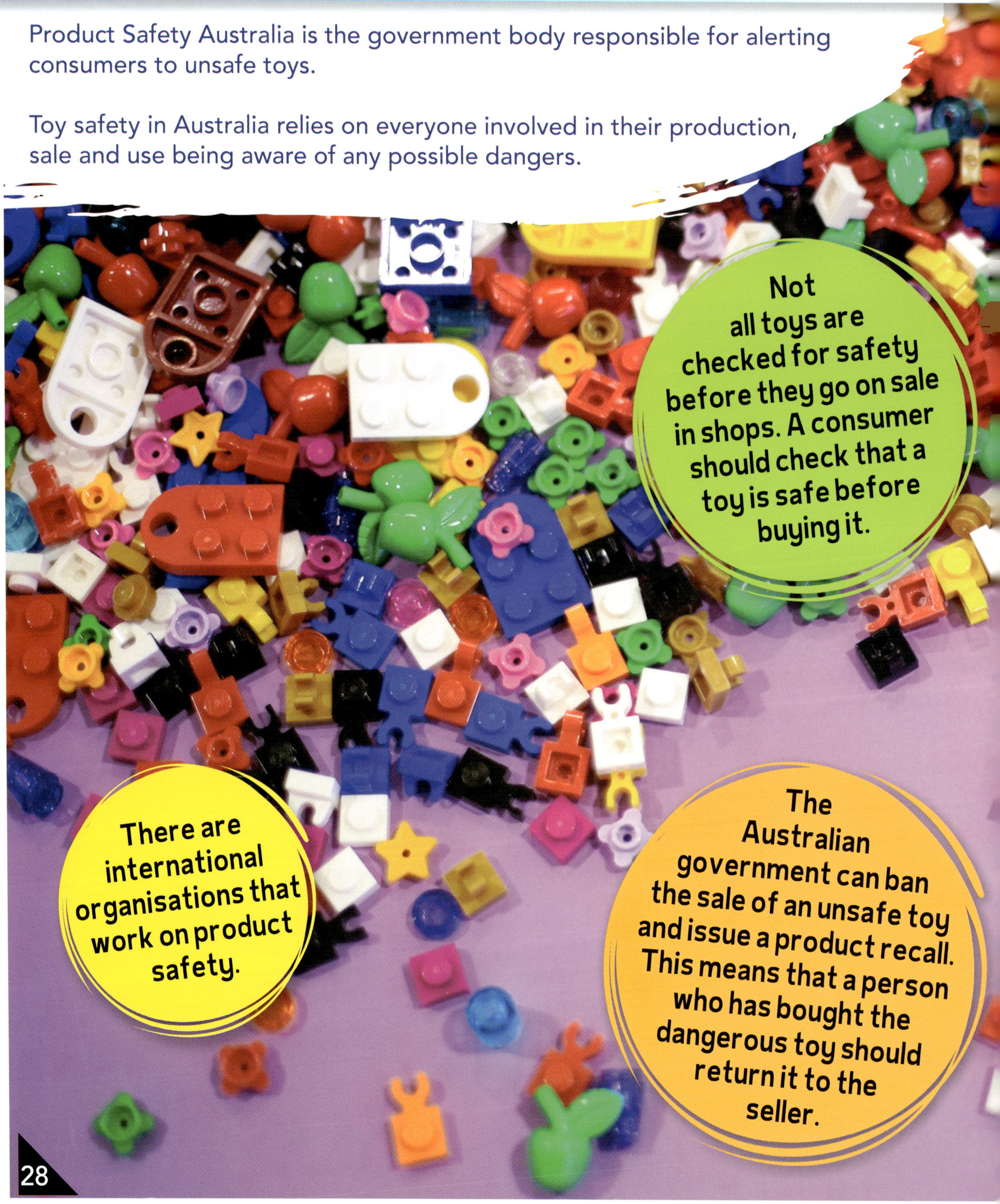

Not all toys are checked for safety before they go on sale in shops. A consumer should check that a toy is safe before buying it.

There are international organisations that work on product safety.

The Australian government can ban the sale of an unsafe toy and issue a product recall. This means that a person who has bought the dangerous toy should return it to the seller.

Here are some of the reasons for toys being declared unsafe in Australia:

The toys contain small batteries or magnets that little children can access and swallow.

The eyes on toys can come off easily and be swallowed.

The toys shoot hard objects that can cause injuries.

The toys contain small beads that children can breathe in or swallow.

The toys contain lead paint or lead as a metal.

There is no warning label about possible dangers.

BUSHFIRES, FLOODS AND CYCLONES

Large scale disasters can be caused by nature or by humans. If you live in an area where bushfires, floods or cyclones may occur, then the adults at home should have a disaster emergency plan.

Emergency service organisations provide information for homeowners on how to be prepared for disasters. Everyone in the house has a role to play in an emergency plan, including the children.

The Australian Broadcasting Commission has a website that lists emergency alerts and warnings for all areas of Australia. It also has plans that people can use to prepare for emergencies in their own area.
www.abc.net.au/news/emergency

Once the disaster is over, it is normal to feel upset. Counselling for adults and children can be a great help when people are trying to overcome their unhappiness after a disaster has affected their lives.

GLOSSARY

arthritis - illness that causes pain in the body's joints
capacitor - device that stores electrical energy
deflate - lose air
ember - small piece of something glowing in a fire
Epipen - medical device used by people with severe allergies
flammable - able to catch alight
geolocator - digital device for finding a location on Earth
GPS - global positioning system
inedible - unable to be eaten
intestines - part of the body that helps digest food
lethal - deadly
microscopic - can only be seen using a microscope
sibling - brother or sister
toddler - child up to about 3 years old

INDEX

Visit these websites to find out more about safety for children:
www.kidshelpline.com.au
www.abc.net.au/news/emergency